First World War
and Army of Occupation
War Diary
France, Belgium and Germany

47 DIVISION
Divisional Troops
Eley Group Royal Artillery Headquarters
1 October 1915 - 31 October 1915

WO95/2718/2

The Naval & Military Press Ltd
www.nmarchive.com
Published in association with The National Archives

Published by

The Naval & Military Press Ltd

Unit 10 Ridgewood Industrial Park,

Uckfield, East Sussex,

TN22 5QE England

Tel: +44 (0) 1825 749494

www.naval-military-press.com

www.nmarchive.com

This diary has been reprinted in facsimile from the original. Any imperfections are inevitably reproduced and the quality may fall short of modern type and cartographic standards.

© **Crown Copyright**
Images reproduced by permission of The National Archives, London, England, 2015.

Contents

Document type	Place/Title	Date From	Date To
Heading	WO95/2718 47 Div Eley Group R.A. HQ Oct 15		
Heading	47th Division Eley Group R.A H.Q. Oct 1915		
War Diary	Les Brebis	01/10/1915	31/10/1915

WO95/2718 (2)

47 DIV
Eley Group R.A. HQ
Oct '15

47TH DIVISION

ELEY GROUP R.A. H.Q.
OCT 1915

Army Form C. 2118.

ELEY GROUP R.A. H.Q.

WAR DIARY
or
INTELLIGENCE SUMMARY.

(Erase heading not required.)

Instructions regarding War Diaries and Intelligence Summaries are contained in F. S. Regs., Part II. and the Staff Manual respectively. Title pages will be prepared in manuscript.

Place	Date	Hour	Summary of Events and Information	Remarks and references to Appendices
LES BREBIS	October 1st		"ELEY" GROUP FORMED: Lt Col E.H. Eley commanding, consisting of 21st, 22nd Btties R.F.A. & 23rd Btty R.G.A. & No 3 Battery Armoured Cars. Batteries improved their gun positions etc. No 1575 Gunner W.E. PHILLIPS posted to Brigade Headquarters.	
	2nd		Germans shelled intermittently throughout the day their old front line held by 5.9" howitzers. The enemy also shelled LOOS, Western end of DOUBLE CRASSIER, our front line trench South of DOUBLE CRASSIER, FOSSE No 5, and NORTH MAROC, with H.E. and shrapnel during the day. 21st Battery post together with his men No.15 H.E.S. Batteries and Headquarters wagon lines, found advanced line at NOEUX LES MINES. Seven rounds were issued and temporarily attached to the Ammunition Column. ELEY	
	3rd	12 noon	Both Batteries opened fire at 12 noon. The 21st Battery expended 200 rounds on trench running South from WOOD 5 and the 22nd Battery expended 157 rounds on WOOD 6. This WOOD was thought to be a strong point in the enemy's line.	
		6.30 pm	At 6.30 pm and 9 pm enemy shelled SOUTH MAROC – M.2.d.8.5. to M.2.a.9.6 — with incendiary shells.	

Eley Group formed. Lt Col E.H. Eley Commanding consisting of 21st 22nd 23rd R.F.A. & No 3 Battery Armoured Cars.

WAR DIARY or INTELLIGENCE SUMMARY

Army Form C. 2118.

Place	Date	Hour	Summary of Events and Information	Remarks and references to Appendices
LES BREBIS.	October 3rd	6pm	Bac: Am: Col: left HAILLICOURT and arrived at NOEUX LES MINES (LES CORONS) at 7.30 p.m. The wagons parked along RUE DE LA CITÉ and the men billeted.	
	4th	11.39am	21st Battery fired 44 rounds for the purpose of bombardment and registration, on trenches East of WOOD 6 (H.31.c.1.5 to H.25.a.0.5.) between 11.39am and 3.24pm	
		7.45pm	At 7.45pm the battery fired 20 rounds on Cié St PIERRE in retaliation for the Germans shelling LOOS. The Bac: Am: Col: received 140 rounds 40 the am from Div: Am: Col: and issued it to the 21st Battery (About 20 shells, mostly china, fell in the vicinity of the water tower in NORTH MAROC, between 9am and 11.30 am possibly from a naval gun fired from an armoured train.	
	5th	1.50pm	The enemy shelled SOUTH MAROC and the 22nd Battery fired 20 rounds in retaliation on Cié St PIERRE. 200 rounds of ammunition for the SHARP Group.	
	6th		21st Battery fired 3 rounds of battery fire on Cié St LAURENT in retaliation for the Germans shelling LOOS. The Germans shelled SOUTH MAROC with heavy stuff during the afternoon and the 22nd Battery retaliated with 20 rounds into Cié St PIERRE. The 22nd Battery fired 16 rounds in registering the following targets. Pits 14 bis West end of WOOD 5. East end of WOOD 5. and track South of WOOD 5.	

Army Form C. 2118.

WAR DIARY
or
INTELLIGENCE SUMMARY.
(Erase heading not required.)

Place	Date	Hour	Summary of Events and Information	Remarks and references to Appendices
LES BREBIS	October 7th		Observation was rendered impossible owing to atmospheric conditions. 31st & 92nd Batteries improved their gun platforms &c:	
	8th.	11.30am	Information was received in the early morning that Germans had our wire in front of their trenches. At 11.30 am, Germans commenced a heavy bombardment of our trenches, this was followed by a counter-attack, along practically the whole of the line captured from them on Sept. 25th. The attack entirely failed on our front. Both batteries were in action during the whole of the day. The 91st Battery engaged trenches and redoubt at H.31.C and a wire hit 70. The fire was very effective. About 50% of the fire was observed our wire hits on enemy's works. The whole of the area in H.33.0 was larger. The total number of rounds fired was 193. 92nd Battery engaged trenches in H.31.b. and H.32.a. the fire [crossed out] very effective, several direct hits being obtained. The area between M.N.12.8.10.8 and N.7.a.8.8, in which were several observation stations and trenches, was thoroughly searched and swept. Barrages were formed between M.S.C.4.1 and M.S.C.5.0, and M.11.a.4.9 and M.11.a.2.9. The total number of rounds fired was 213. The Bde. Amn: Col: received 365 rds. of 50lb Amm. from the Div: Amn: Col:	

1577 Wt. W10791/1773 500,000 1/15 D.D. & L. A.D.S.S./Forms/C. 2118.

WAR DIARY
or
INTELLIGENCE SUMMARY

Army Form C. 2118.

Place	Date	Hour	Summary of Events and Information	Remarks and references to Appendices
LES BREBIS	October 9th		During the afternoon SOUTH MAROC was shelled by German high velocity guns with phosphor shells. The 22nd Battery fired in retaliation 45 rounds into Co St. PIERRE, at 5 pm.	
		5pm	At 5.30 pm a considerable number of large H.E. Shells fell in front of the Battery apparently intended for the communication trench leading to the railway cutting. The Battery fired 8 rounds in retaliation on Cité St LAURENT at 9.15 pm. 21st Battery fired 21 rounds into Cité St LAURENT and 67 into Cité Cité St AUGUSTE in retaliation for German shelling. LOSS. The Bav. [illegible] number 220 rounds to 21st Battery and 36 rounds to 22nd Battery	
	10th	3pm	The 21st Battery fired 9 rounds for registration purposes on trench H.19.a.5.0.— H.19.c.9.6. [illegible]. 4 of the rounds were blinds.	
		4pm	The Germans shelled MAROC with H.E. shell. Both batteries retaliated – the 21st Battery firing on enemy battery on M.11.b.8.55 and M.12.a.38 and the 22nd Battery on Cité St. PIERRE.	
			The 22nd Battery fired 18 rounds in registering the enemy's front line trench from H.19.a.4.3 to H.19.c.9.6. – 2 direct hits were obtained. The Bombardier	

WAR DIARY
or
INTELLIGENCE SUMMARY.

(Erase heading not required.)

Army Form C. 2118.

Place	Date	Hour	Summary of Events and Information	Remarks and references to Appendices
LES BREBIS	October 10th		The Adv. Am. Col. recepts 90 rounds of 50 lb shell from Division which was issued to 21st Battery and 40 lb shell and 90 rounds of 50 lb shell was received from HQ. Am. Col. and issued to 22nd Battery	
			21st Battery 5.3 was issued 30lb shell from Division on the morning 5/10/15. Both batteries	
	11th		The French attempted to retake a short length of trench lost on 5/10/15.	
	2 pm		Supported the attack which failed. The 21st Battery fired 1149 rounds on enemy trenches along the railway at M.6.c. 4.6.3. 8 rounds were fired on an enemy battery at M.16.b.13.9 and at 3.30 pm fire was shifted back to the trenches along the railway.	
	4.2 pm		21 rounds were fired on trenches in Cite St. PIERRE and again at 4.5 pm 57 rounds were fired on to the same trenches.	
	2 pm		22nd Battery opened fire & 101 rounds on the trench along the railway at M.G.C.9.25 and on trenches and billets in Cite St. PIERRE. At 2.27 pm the fire was shifted on to enemy battery positions in M.11.6.8.1. 9 rounds along fired. At 2.30 pm the fire was shifted	
	2.47 pm			
	2.50 pm		back on to the original targets and 10 rounds fired. The communication trench at the Eastern end of DOUBLE CRASSIER (including FOSSE No 11) enemy batteries in M.10.6.2.8.) were engaged alternately and M.10.6.8.1. and M.18.a.2.8., 4.9.3, 7.9.3 and 6.6. were engaged alternately, and the original targets. Viz.: trench along railway and trenches and billets in Cite St. PIERRE. Total number of rounds fired by 22nd Battery was 432.	

Army Form C. 2118.

WAR DIARY
or
INTELLIGENCE SUMMARY.
(Erase heading not required.)

Place	Date	Hour	Summary of Events and Information	Remarks and references to Appendices
LES BREBIS	October 11th		2/Lieuts: T. CAULFEILD STOKER and G.A.E. STEPHENSON with 15 O.Rs from 3rd/1st London (Res) F.A. Res: arrived from the Base. Base: Ammrs and both batteries had 5 men each attached to them. 2/Lt. T. CAULFEILD STOKER attached to the 21st Battery and 2/Lt. G.A.E. STEPHENSON attached to the 22nd Battery. These officers were afterwards posted to the respective batteries, supernumerary to establishment. No rea The Bde: Amn: Col: received 89 rounds of 4.5" shell from the 10th Amn: Col: and issued 750 rounds to the 21st Battery.	
	12th.	4.3pm	21st Battery fired 3 rounds on Cite St. PIERRE in retaliation for enemy shelling MAROC. A fire was started in that village by our shells, which lasted for 3 days. 21st Battery fired 19 rounds on German front line trench at H.9.a.32. in	
		4.26 pm	retaliation for enemy shelling our front line trenches. At 8.30pm battery fires 15	
		8.30pm	rounds on Cite St. PIERRE in retaliation for enemy shelling LOOS. The 22nd Battery fired 96 rounds and registered the trench in H.19.a.I.0. The Bde: Am: Col: received 489 rounds 4.5 Shell from the Am: Col: and 259 rounds 4.5 Shells issued to 22nd Battery. 251 rounds 4.5 shell received from 21st Battery and returned to Divi: Am: Col.	

Army Form C. 2118.

WAR DIARY
or
INTELLIGENCE SUMMARY
(Erase heading not required.)

Place	Date	Hour	Summary of Events and Information	Remarks and references to Appendices
LES BREBIS	October 13th	12.30pm	All Batteries supported an attack, the objective being the L.T.B. Rd. & outskirts of Hulluch from LaBassée ~~~~~~~~~~~ Fire ordered 12.30pm. The 21st Battery firing 117 rounds and the 22nd Battery 164 rounds on German front	
		2pm	line trenches at H.19.a.1.3 to H.19.a.P.1. At 2pm 148 rounds were fired by 21st Battery on trenches and HOODS 3 H and G. The 22nd Battery fired 282 rounds on	
		4.46pm	German trenches H.19.a.2.0.6 H.19.a.5.2. At 4.46pm the 21st Battery changed their fire to first line trench from H.19.a.1.3. to H.19.a.5.1. These guns only were in action, and during the first period, the only fire being	
		5.8pm to 8pm	three broken shrap shot charges. At 5.8pm the 22nd Battery formed a barrage between H.19.c.F.5. to H.19.a.0.5. expending 29 rounds. Bde. Am. Col. received 606 rounds of 40H Shell from the Bde. Am. Col. and issued 403 rounds to 21st Battery. 5.506 Shells were received from 22nd Battery and were returned to Bde. Am. Col.	
	14th		22nd Battery did not fire. 21st Battery fired 9 rounds on the St. LAURENT-in ~~illegible~~ for German Trenches ~~illegible~~ and 249 sols from one. Bde. Am. Col. received 317 rounds 40H Shell and about 208 rounds to 21st Battery and 240 rounds 9 Shot to 22nd Battery, 14 506 Shell issued to 22nd Battery	

Army Form C. 2118.

WAR DIARY
or
INTELLIGENCE SUMMARY.

(Erase heading not required.)

Instructions regarding War Diaries and Intelligence Summaries are contained in F.S. Regs., Part II. and the Staff Manual respectively. Title pages will be prepared in manuscript.

Place	Date	Hour	Summary of Events and Information	Remarks and references to Appendices
LES BREBIS	October 15th		SOUTH MAROC was slightly shelled during the afternoon by light high velocity field guns.	
	16		Batteries did not fire. Improvements were carried out to gun positions etc:	
	17th		Germans shelled SOUTH MAROC. 22nd Battery retaliated by firing 5 rounds into Cité St. PIERRE. Batt: Am: Col: Supplied 2 wagons and 13 men to R.E. fatigues.	
	18		Bt. Bde: reconnoitred positions for batteries in vicinity of G.27.C. Germans shelled SOUTH MAROC and both batteries retaliated — 21st Battery firing 51 rounds into Cité St. PIERRE and the 22nd Battery firing 49 rounds into WOOD 5 and 5 rounds into Cité St. PIERRE. Batt: Am: Col: received 109 rounds of 40 lb shell from Bois Hon. Col: and wooded as that 40 lb shell to 21st Battery and 45 rounds 50 lb shell to 22nd Battery	
	19th	3pm	During the afternoon MAROC was shelled. Both batteries retaliated by firing 6 rounds into Cité St. PIERRE and the 21 st Battery fired 13 rounds on the	
		7.30pm	trenches in BOIS HUGO. At 7.30pm 21 st Battery fired 4 rounds, again in retaliation for shelling MAROC, into Cité St. PIERRE.	
	20th	12 noon	Both Batteries engaged enemy trench H.25.d.f.10.3b H.19.d.4.o.32 rounds being	
		1.15pm	expended by each battery. At 1.15 pm. each battery fired 12 rounds into	
		4pm	WOOD 5 and WOOD 4 & WOOD 3. At 4pm 22nd battery shelled WOOD 6 with	

Army Form C. 2118.

WAR DIARY
or
INTELLIGENCE SUMMARY.
(Erase heading not required.)

Place	Date	Hour	Summary of Events and Information	Remarks and references to Appendices
LES BREBIS	October 20th		15 rounds. The right section of 22nd Battery moved to Fosse No 7.	2/Lt ... ...
			Bde. Am. Col. issued 60 rounds of 3.9 and 7? rounds of 5.0 shell to 21st Battery and 60 rounds of 40 to 21st and 6 to 22nd Battery.	10th Cpl. Harris having been ... replaced to Bde Signal authority office.
	21st	2 pm	Both Batteries fired 32 rounds on German front line trench at H.Q.a.5.0 & H.9.a.6.5 in retaliation for enemy shelling our front line trenches. The right section of	
		3.34 pm	22nd Battery registered Pts 15 & 16 at 3.34pm. In the evening the left section moved to Fosse No 7.	
			The Bde. Am. Col. commenced instruction in signalling for & N.C.O.'s since then.	
			101 rounds 40th still took account from the Bde. Am. Col. 40 rounds of what were issued to 21st Battery.	
	22nd	12.22 pm	Germans shelled LOOS and the CHALK PIT during the day. The 21st Battery fired 4 rounds on WOODS & ANS. in retaliation and 22nd Battery fired 12 rounds	
		1.59	until St AUGUSTE. 21st Battery fired 8 rounds until St AUGUSTE.	
		4 pm	The Germans shelled the whole British front line. Both batteries retaliated by shelling Rte. St. AUGUSTE. At 10 am. 40th Battery R.F.A. was brigaded with the E.F.J Group	
			Bde. Am. Col. issued 112 rounds of 18 p.r. ... Shell and 20 rounds of 4.5 ... Shell issued to 21st Battery, 35 rounds 50 to ... assumed command of Battery from Major Crawe. received from Div. Par Park.	Major F. Eley assumed command of the Bde.

Lt.Col. E.H. ELEY granted 7 days leave of absence.

Army Form C. 2118.

WAR DIARY
or
INTELLIGENCE SUMMARY.
(Erase heading not required.)

Instructions regarding War Diaries and Intelligence Summaries are contained in F. S. Regs., Part II. and the Staff Manual respectively. Title pages will be prepared in manuscript.

Place	Date	Hour	Summary of Events and Information	Remarks and references to Appendices
LES BREBIS.	October 23rd	1.10pm	D.1.A. Battery fired 20 rounds on Cité St. AUGUSTE in retaliation for Germans shelling CHALK PIT.	
		3.40pm	At 3.40pm 22nd Battery fired 4 rounds on FERME DES MINES in retaliation for enemy shelling CHALK PIT and 8 rounds on Cité St. AUGUSTE for shelling LOOS. Left section registered on PITS 14 bis. 23rd Siege Battery left ELEY Group. Lieutenant Lt. J.W. HENDERSON of the 3/8th London (How) F.A. Bde. joined Brigade from Base and was posted to 2/1st Battery. Supernumerary to establishment. [struck through text] 2nd Battery [struck through text]	
	24th	2.10pm	During the day LOOS was shelled by the Germans. Both batteries retaliated by firing 8 rounds each on Cité St. AUGUSTE. 10 rounds were fired by 22nd Battery on German front line trenches at H.32.a.4.2 in retaliation for enemy shelling our front line trenches at 4pm.	
		4pm	21st Battery fired 28 rounds on trench H.25.4.4.5. and trenches from H.25.b.5.10. to H.25.b.7.7. in retaliation for Germans shelling our trenches. After our 4pm firing, the enemy retaliated slightly on LOOS and CHALK PIT WOOD.	

WAR DIARY or INTELLIGENCE SUMMARY

Army Form C. 2118.

Place	Date	Hour	Summary of Events and Information	Remarks and references to Appendices
LES BREBIS	October			
	24th		Lieut. Rm. Col. received 43 rounds 40th batt. from Sec. Rm. Col. and fired 10 rounds to 21st Battery.	
	25th	11a.m.	Each battery bombarded enemy's second line trench from H.13.b.1.2 to H.13.a.9.4 with 8 rounds per gun. At 11.10 am this was repeated and again at 11.20 am when 4 rounds per gun were fired in salvos.	
		4.10pm	21st Battery fired on Cité St AUGUSTE in retaliation for enemy shelling CHALK PIT and at the same time 22nd Battery fired 16 rounds on same place in retaliation for enemy shelling Loos with 5.9" howitzers — many hits. At 4.25 pm. 21st Battery fired 8 rounds	
		4.25pm	into Cité St AUGUSTE in retaliation for enemy shelling Loos and our front line trenches. Major Bell Irvine leave to England. Major Von Assumes command. Lieut. Rm. Col. received 43 rounds of 40th shell from Sec. Rm. Col. and fired 50 rounds to 21st Battery and 6 rounds to 22nd Battery.	
	26th		22nd Battery registered one section on Redoubt in A.20.d and one section on enemy's trenches. Germans shelled front line trenches from CHALK PIT to LOOS with light field guns and the vicinity between	

Army Form C. 2118.

WAR DIARY
or
INTELLIGENCE SUMMARY.
(Erase heading not required.)

Place	Date	Hour	Summary of Events and Information	Remarks and references to Appendices
LES BREBIS	Oct: 26th		LES BREBIS and FOSSE N°7 with howitzer guns. Both batteries retaliated.	
		12.30pm	21st Battery fired 1 round on Cité St LAURENT and at 12.50pm 20 rounds on trenches in Cité St AUGUSTE. During the afternoon 21st Battery fired 48 rounds on Cité St LAURENT and trenches round WOOD 4.5, and 6.	
		2.20pm		
		2.29pm	The 22nd Battery fired 20 rounds on enemy's front line trench at H.25.b.5.5 & H.25.V.5.4.10. Bee Ambl received 206 rounds of 4.0lb shell from Bos Control and round 48 rounds to 1st Battery and 72nd to 22nd Battery. 20 N.C.O's men were supplied for working party for evening hasty improvements. During the morning German shelled LOOS and our trenches. Both batteries retaliated — the 1st Battery firing 26 rounds on BOIS H.50 and the 22nd Battery 12 rounds on WOOD 3. At 12.25 pm	
	27th	12.21	Cité St LAURENT and the 22nd Battery 12 rounds on WOOD 3. Germans again shelled LOOS. This time both batteries retaliated on Cité St AUGUSTE firing 16 and 15 rounds respectively. Late in the afternoon	
		3pm	Germans shelled our front line trenches and LOOS for which retaliation was carried out on trenches round WOOD 6 and Cité St LAURENT.	

WAR DIARY or INTELLIGENCE SUMMARY

Army Form C. 2118.

Place	Date	Hour	Summary of Events and Information	Remarks and references to Appendices
LES BREBIS	Feb. 27th		Bde: Amn: Col: issued 89 rounds of Staff Shell to 21st Battery and 62 rounds of Lott Shell; 48 S.T. rounds & 40 Shell were drawn from Bde Amn: Col: and 30 rounds issued to 2nd Battery. 120 Mad men were sent out for shooting Party.	
	28th	9 am	Germans shelled our front line trenches: Retaliation was carried out on German trenches North and South of Posts 14 & 15. An Observation Station having been located at H.32.a.6.2. 12 rounds were fired into it by 21st Battery. At 2.30 pm fired 6 rounds on Observation Station at H.31.b.6.0 in retaliation for enemy shelling our front trenches.	
		2.30 pm	Enemy fired 11 rounds of 5.9" Shell at MAROC Church.	
		4.30 pm	Bde: Amn: Col: received 210 rounds 40 to Shell from Bde Amn Col - 145 rounds were issued to 21st Battery and 132 rounds to 2nd Battery. 10 N Cos men were sent out supplies for shooting Party.	
	29th	6.30 am	During the morning the Germans shelled the copse pit. Retaliation was carried out by both batteries with 5 rounds each on pit at PIERRE and H.26.a.0.3. At 12.42 pm. 21st Battery fired 23 rounds on H.31.b.6.3.0 in retaliation for Germans shelling our front line trenches.	
		12.42 pm		

WAR DIARY
or
INTELLIGENCE SUMMARY
(Erase heading not required.)

Army Form C. 2118.

Place	Date	Hour	Summary of Events and Information	Remarks and references to Appendices
LES BREBIS	Feb: 20th	2.10pm	21st Battery fired 12 rounds on German front line right of the Cemetery.	
		3pm	Enemy again shelled CHALK PIT and front trenches. Retaliation was carried out by a slow bombardment by both batteries on HOOD 6, trenches at H.19.a.23. Ema Pts 14 bis.	
			18th Ami. Col. received 114 rounds from Bns' Am Col and issued 78 rounds to 21st Battery and 40 rounds to 22nd Battery. 10 WOO omen were supplied for working party at the building huts. Remount was received.	
			Lt. Col. E.H. ELEY returned from leave and resumed command of Groupement.	
	21st	9am	Brigade. At 9am, 21st Battery retaliated with 16 rounds on BOIS HUGO for enemy shelling our front line trenches. During the greater part of the morning the Germans continued this shelling, both batteries retaliating on BOIS HUGO. Lieut de AUGUSTE and Pts 14 bis. During the afternoon the Germans shelled LOOS and the CHALK PIT. Retaliation was carried out on Ile de LAURENT, and trenches around HOOD 6 and HOOD 7.	
		3pm	A slow bombardment was carried out on German lines as follows:-	

Army Form C. 2118.

WAR DIARY
or
INTELLIGENCE SUMMARY.
(Erase heading not required.)

Instructions regarding War Diaries and Intelligence Summaries are contained in F.S. Regs., Part II. and the Staff Manual respectively. Title pages will be prepared in manuscript.

Place	Date	Hour	Summary of Events and Information	Remarks and references to Appendices
LES BREBIS	Oct: 2nd	8/pm	21st Battery - 16 rounds on trenches H.19.8.02. to H.9.5.10.6.	
			2nd Battery - 16 rounds on trench H.9.a.9d.	
			Bde: Am: Col: received 961 rounds 4.5" shell from Ni:m Col: and issued 784 rounds to 21st and 30 rounds to 2nd to 21st Battery and 112 Bois and 186 box cart: plg.	
		3rd:	10 men were employed forklonding party.	
			During the whole day the Germans shelled LOOS and our trenches. Retaliation was carried out as follows:- At 10.34 am 21st Battery fired 4 rounds on	
		12.3pm	Cité St LAURENT, and at 12.21pm 1 round on trench West of WOOD 6.	
		1.2pm	St AUBERT. The 22nd Battery fires 4 rounds in trench in H.26.a.00	
			16 rounds were fired during the afternoon of Cité St PIERRE and in retaliation for German shelling LOOS and fired 10 rounds at Cité St AUBERT	
		3.25pm	Battery fired 22 rounds on enemy's trenches round Pits in H.9.a during the rest of the afternoon.	
			Bde: Am: Col: received 98 rounds of 4.5" shell from Res: Am Col: and issued 91 rounds to 2nd Battery and retained 88 to 22nd and 150 to 21st Battery. 10 men employed for working party.	

1577 Wt. W10791/1773 500,000 1/15 D.D.&L. A.D.S.S./Forms/C. 2118.

www.ingramcontent.com/pod-product-compliance
Lightning Source LLC
Chambersburg PA
CBHW081253170426
43191CB00037B/2138